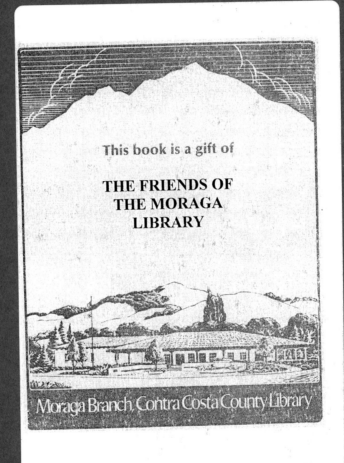

THE BEST
DOGS
EVER

LABRADOR RETRIEVERS ARE THE BEST!

Elaine Landau

LERNER PUBLICATIONS COMPANY · MINNEAPOLIS

For Terry Young

Lerner Publications Company
A division of Lerner Publishing Group, Inc.
241 First Avenue North
Minneapolis, MN 55401 U.S.A.

Website address: www.lernerbooks.com

Library of Congress Cataloging-in-Publication Data

Landau, Elaine.
    Labrador retrievers are the best! / by Elaine Landau.
       p.   cm. – (The best dogs ever)
    Includes index.
    ISBN 978-1-58013-556-6 (lib. bdg. : alk. paper)
    1. Labrador retriever—Juvenile literature. I. Title.
  SF429.L3L38 2010
  636.752'7–dc22   2008046791

Manufactured in the United States of America
1 2 3 4 5 6 - BP - 15 14 13 12 11 10

TABLE OF CONTENTS

CHAPTER ONE

THE PERFECT DOG

Picture the perfect dog. Is it a sweet, loving, playful pooch? Perhaps you prefer a highly intelligent dog. How about a dog that is eager to please?

Maybe all these things appeal to you. Then you might want a Labrador retriever. **Labrador retrievers** are also known as Labs. They have often been called the perfect pet as well.

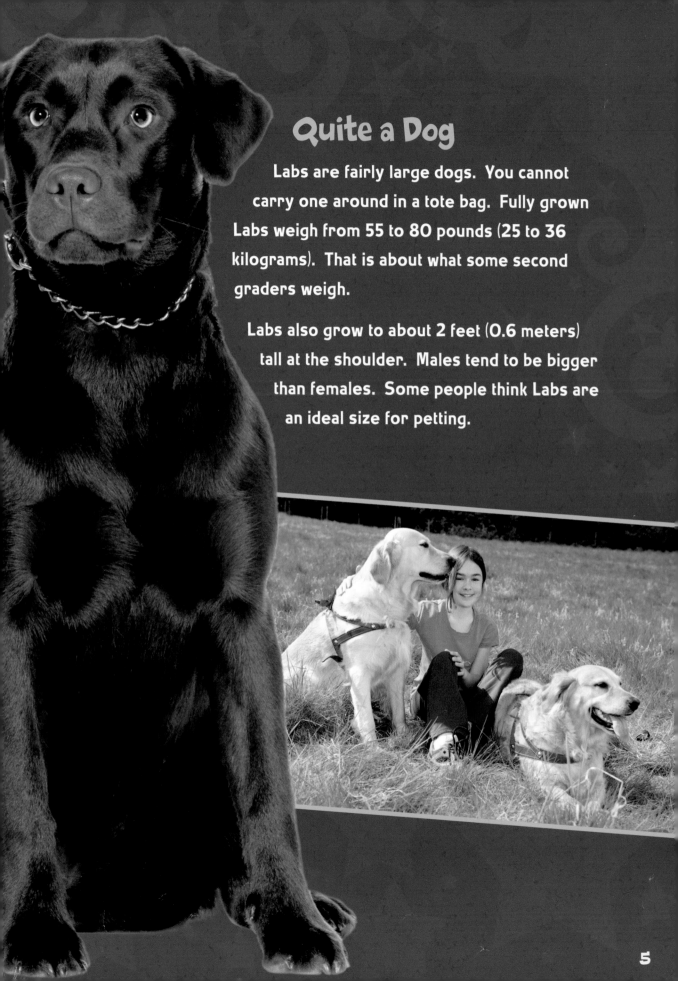

Quite a Dog

Labs are fairly large dogs. You cannot carry one around in a tote bag. Fully grown Labs weigh from 55 to 80 pounds (25 to 36 kilograms). That is about what some second graders weigh.

Labs also grow to about 2 feet (0.6 meters) tall at the shoulder. Males tend to be bigger than females. Some people think Labs are an ideal size for petting.

WHAT TO NAME YOUR LABRADOR RETRIEVER

Thinking about names for your new Lab? Here are a few that might do:

Astro

Harley

Nikki

Goldie
(for a yellow Lab)

JAKE

maggie

velvet
(for a black Lab)

Magic

COCOA
(for a chocolate brown Lab)

FLASH

Fit as a Fiddle and Ready for Fun

Labrador retrievers do not lack pep. These pooches have lots of energy. They are ready for fun when you are.

Labs love to go for long walks. They also enjoy a good run outdoors. They will play fetch with you any day of the week.

A RETRIEVING DOG

Retrieve means to "bring something back." So it's no surprise that Labrador retrievers like to retrieve toys their owners throw!

Colorful Coats

Labs come in several colors. You can get a black, yellow, or chocolate brown one. All have short, thick coats. That makes them easy to groom.

Labs' coats are waterproof too. This is important because Labs love water. They will swim with you and play water games. Labs even have webbed feet! Webbed feet help the dogs swim.

Labs love to hang out with kids. They make great friends.

A Popular Pooch

Labrador retrievers are among the most popular dogs in the United States. It is easy to see why. Few dogs are as outgoing, friendly, or gentle.

Labs are great with both kids and adults. They do well around other pets too. But most of all, these dogs love being with their owners. Lab owners usually get lots of warm, wet doggie kisses.

Lab owners often feel they have the best dog ever. Who can blame them? If you had a Labrador retriever, you just might feel the same way.

A SPECIAL WHITE HOUSE DOG

Former president Bill Clinton had a chocolate brown Lab named Buddy. Buddy was often seen playing on the White House lawn. He'd happily leap into the president's helicopter for a ride with Clinton. Some say Buddy was the most photographed dog in the country.

President Bill Clinton sits with his chocolate Labrador retriever, Buddy, in 1997.

9

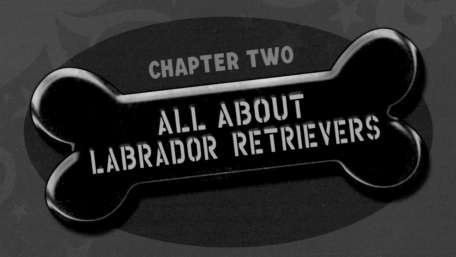

CHAPTER TWO
ALL ABOUT LABRADOR RETRIEVERS

Dogs and humans are a good match. Dogs are both our helpers and our friends. It's been that way for thousands of years.

DOGS IN ANCIENT TIMES

The ancient Romans used dogs in their army. Some were trained as attack dogs. Other dogs learned to carry messages. Still others were used as guard dogs.

The ancient Egyptians had guard dogs too. The dogs were often taken on hunting trips. Archaeologists—scientists who learn about the past by digging up old objects—have even found dog mummies buried in their owners' tombs.

Dog Groups

These days, there are many types of dogs. The American Kennel Club (AKC) groups the different types by breed. Breeds with similar features are grouped together. Some of the AKC's groups include the hound group, the working group, and the toy group.

This Afghan hound is in the hound group.

Yorkshire terriers are in the toy group.

This boxer belongs to the working group.

Labs are in the sporting group. Dogs in the sporting group tend to be active and alert. These dogs need lots of exercise. They do well in both the water and the woods. All sporting dogs are good hunters.

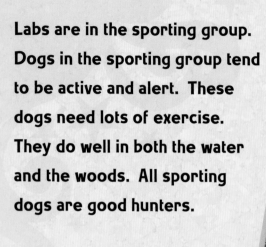

This black Lab runs after a bird as his owner hunts.

THE SPORTING GROUP

The sporting group includes twenty-seven dog breeds. You've probably heard of some of them. Cocker spaniels, pointers, and Irish setters (right) are in the sporting group.

The Labrador Retriever's History

Labs come from Newfoundland, Canada. That is a cold, windy island surrounded by icy waters. Settlers in Newfoundland began fishing those icy waters hundreds of years ago.

By the late 1600s, Labs were working with these settlers. The dogs pulled in fishing nets. They also went after fish that escaped from the nets.

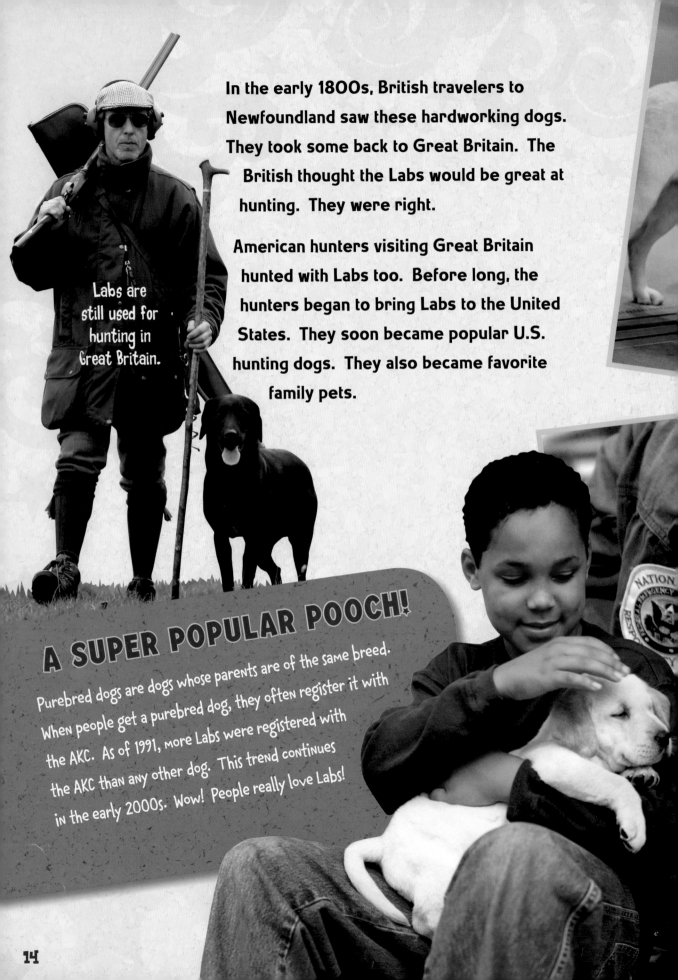

In the early 1800s, British travelers to Newfoundland saw these hardworking dogs. They took some back to Great Britain. The British thought the Labs would be great at hunting. They were right.

American hunters visiting Great Britain hunted with Labs too. Before long, the hunters began to bring Labs to the United States. They soon became popular U.S. hunting dogs. They also became favorite family pets.

Labs are still used for hunting in Great Britain.

A SUPER POPULAR POOCH!

Purebred dogs are dogs whose parents are of the same breed. When people get a purebred dog, they often register it with the AKC. As of 1991, more Labs were registered with the AKC than any other dog. This trend continues in the early 2000s. Wow! People really love Labs!

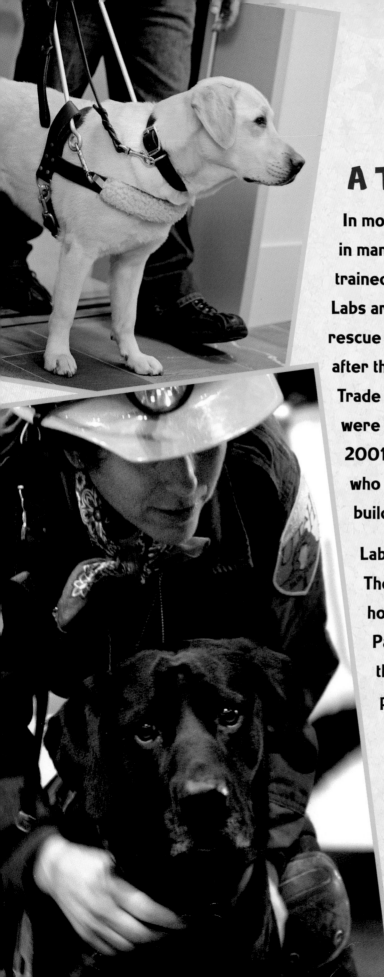

A True Service Dog

In modern times, Labs help humans in many ways. They are often trained as guide dogs for the blind. Labs are also used for search and rescue missions. The dogs helped after the Twin Towers of the World Trade Center in New York City were destroyed on September 11, 2001. They searched for people who were trapped beneath the buildings' rubble.

Labs also serve as therapy dogs. Therapy dogs are brought to hospitals or nursing homes. Patients pet and play with them. These dogs brighten the patients' days.

Top: This yellow Lab works as a guide dog for its blind owner. *Left:* This black Lab helped search the World Trade Center site after September 11, 2001.

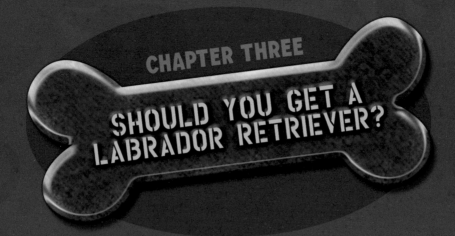

CHAPTER THREE

SHOULD YOU GET A LABRADOR RETRIEVER?

Have you ever heard this joke?

Question:
Why are bananas my favorite fruit?

Answer:
Because they have appeal.

Labs have appeal too. Yet they may not be right for everyone. Picking the wrong dog is no joke.

Is a Lab Right for You?

Labs are large. Lots of people like a huge pooch. Yet is bigger always better?

Large dogs have some special needs. One of these is space. Labs need room to stretch out and move around. A big dog in a small space can easily knock things over.

WELCOME TO YOUR NEW HOME!

How old should your Lab puppy be before you bring it home? Take this quiz to see if you know.

A. 4 weeks

B. 6 weeks

C. 8 weeks

The correct answer is C. A Lab puppy should stay with its mother for the first 8 weeks of its life. It needs this time to learn from its mother and to nurse (drink its mother's milk). Nursing helps puppies grow.

Labs are also quite active. They need to exercise. A big backyard is ideal for a Lab. Living near a park or an open field is good too.

But what if you live in a small apartment in a city? Are the streets where you live crowded? Would it be hard to take a big dog for a brisk walk there? If this sounds like your neighborhood, a small dog might be better for you.

Labs do best when they have lots of room to run around.

Time with Your Lab

Labs also need lots of attention. They should not be left alone most of the day. If that happens, they sometimes develop behavior problems.

Lab owners need time to pet and play with their dog. Do you have lots of after-school activities? Are you hardly ever home? If the answer to these questions is yes, then a Lab might not be right for you.

MISCHIEVOUS LABS

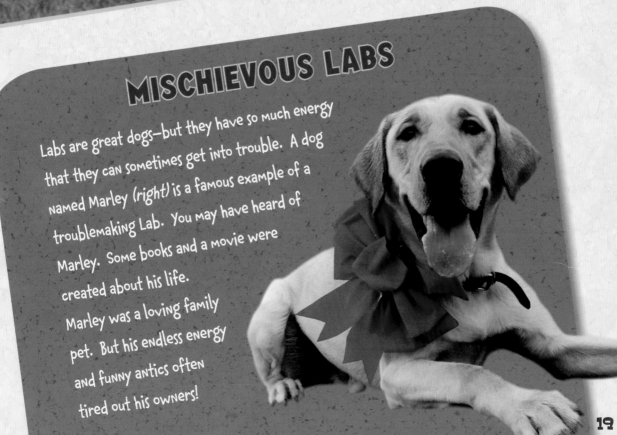

Labs are great dogs—but they have so much energy that they can sometimes get into trouble. A dog named Marley (right) is a famous example of a troublemaking Lab. You may have heard of Marley. Some books and a movie were created about his life. Marley was a loving family pet. But his endless energy and funny antics often tired out his owners!

Feeding Time

Big dogs are big eaters. Feeding
a Lab can be costly. Talk this over
with an adult in your family. Find
out if you can afford a big dog.

PUPPIES ARE CUTE, BUT...

Should you get a puppy? Or would a full-grown Lab be better for you? Puppies are cute, but they are a lot of work.

Puppies must be fed four times a day. They also have to be housebroken. Training a young dog takes a lot of time and patience. It means a lot more cleaning up too!

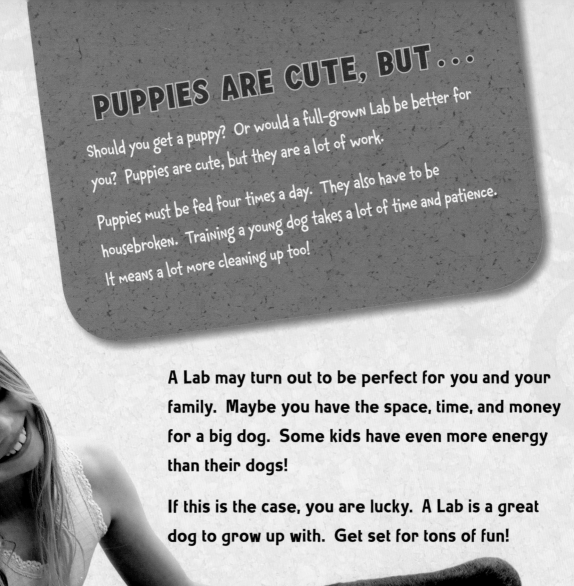

A Lab may turn out to be perfect for you and your family. Maybe you have the space, time, and money for a big dog. Some kids have even more energy than their dogs!

If this is the case, you are lucky. A Lab is a great dog to grow up with. Get set for tons of fun!

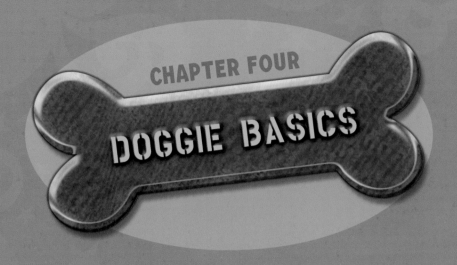

CHAPTER FOUR

DOGGIE BASICS

What an exciting day! Your Lab is coming home. Make sure you are ready for your newest family member.

A Visit to the Vet

When you bring your dog home, you'll want to make an appointment with a pet doctor, or veterinarian (also called a vet). The vet will examine your dog for health problems. Your dog will also get the shots it needs to prevent diseases.

Bring your Lab back to the vet for regular checkups. Also take your dog to the vet if it becomes ill. After you, your vet may be your dog's best friend.

Be Prepared!

Every dog needs some basic supplies in its new home. Here's a short list of things to get you started:

collar

leash

tags (for identification)

dog food

food and water bowls

crates (one for when your pet travels by car and one for it to rest in at home)

treats (to be used in training)

toys

It's important for your Lab to wear a collar and ID tags. Tags help identify dogs if they get lost.

WONDERFUL WATER!

All living things need water. Water is even more important than food. Make sure your dog always has a bowl of fresh, cool water. Change the water twice daily and keep the bowl clean. You'll be helping your dog stay healthy and happy!

Dog food is an especially important item on the list. Be sure to feed your Lab a high-quality food. There are different foods for puppies and for full-grown dogs. Ask your vet which food is best.

Grooming

All dogs need to be groomed. Labs do not require a great deal of grooming. However, you should brush your Lab's coat every day. This will remove any dead skin and fur. It will also make your dog's fur shine.

Exercise and Fun

Dogs need plenty of exercise. And Labs love to play! Often their owners do too. Exercise can be great for both of you. Take long walks with your Lab. Play fetch. Have some fun with a Frisbee. Swim with your Lab as well.

You can also buy dog toys for your Lab. Toys will keep your Lab happy and busy. Just be sure the toys you pick are safe and are made for a large dog.

Labs love to go for walks. Walking or running with your Lab is one way to spend time with your dog and give it some exercise.

Love Your Lab

Your Lab will always look to you for care and love. Don't let your pooch down. Getting a dog is a big responsibility. A dog needs attention and care even when you are tired or busy.

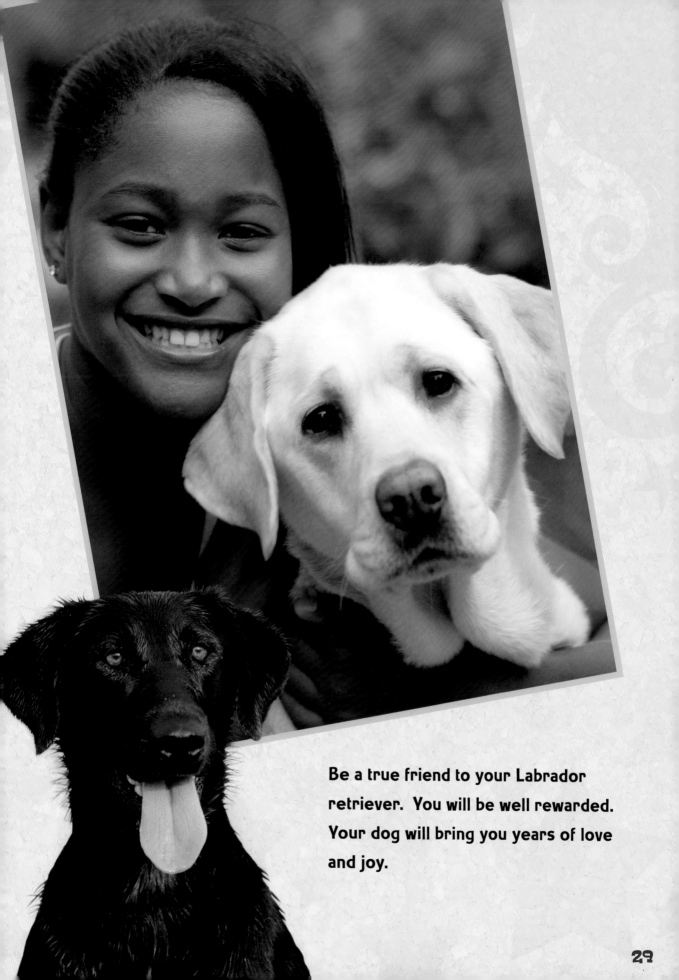

Be a true friend to your Labrador retriever. You will be well rewarded. Your dog will bring you years of love and joy.

GLOSSARY

American Kennel Club (AKC): an organization that groups dogs by breed. The AKC also defines the characteristics of different breeds.

breed: a particular type of dog. Dogs of the same breed have the same body shape and general features.

coat: a dog's fur

groom: to clean, brush, and trim a dog's coat

guide dog: a dog used to lead people who have trouble seeing or who are blind

nurse: to drink a mother's milk

purebred: a dog whose parents are of the same breed

retrieve: to bring something back

sporting group: a group of dogs that tend to be active and alert. Dogs in the sporting group make good hunters.

therapy dog: a dog brought to nursing homes or hospitals to comfort patients

veterinarian: a doctor who treats animals. Veterinarians are called vets for short.

webbed: connected by a web or fold of skin

FOR MORE INFORMATION

Books

Brecke, Nicole, and Patricia M. Stockland. *Dogs You Can Draw*. Minneapolis: Millbrook Press, 2010. Brecke and Stockland show how to draw many different dog breeds, including the Labrador retriever.

Gray, Susan H. *Labradors*. Chanhassen, MN: Child's World, 2007. Readers will find a close-up look at Labrador retrievers in this book.

MacAulay, Kelley, and Bobbie Kalman. *Labrador Retrievers*. New York: Crabtree, 2007. This book for Lab lovers includes information on grooming, feeding, and exercising Labs.

Markle, Sandra. *Animal Heroes: True Rescue Stories*. Minneapolis: Millbrook Press, 2009. Markle tells how dogs, cats, monkeys, and other animals have saved humans from dangerous situations.

McDaniel, Melissa. *Guide Dogs*. New York: Bearport, 2005. This book features stories of real dogs helping their human companions. It provides a good look at Labs doing what they do best.

Websites

American Kennel Club
http://www.akc.org
Visit this website to find a complete listing of AKC-registered dog breeds, including the Labrador retriever. This site also features fun printable activities for kids.

ASPCA Animaland
http://www.aspca.org/site/PageServer?pagename=kids_pc_home
Check out this page for helpful hints on caring for a dog and other pets.

Index

Photo Acknowledgments

The images in this book are used with the permission of: backgrounds © iStockphoto.com/Julie Fisher and © iStockphoto.com/Tomasz Adamczyk; © iStockphoto.com/Michael Balderas, p. 1; © Nicholas Russell/The Image Bank/Getty Images, p. 4; © Eric Isselée/Dreamstime.com, p. 5 (left); © Jacek Chabraszewski/Dreamstime.com, p. 5 (right); © Martin Valigursky/Dreamstime.com, p. 6; © Callalloo Candcy-Fotolia.com, p. 7; © Steve Smith/Taxi/Getty Images, p. 8; © Photononstop/SuperStock, pp. 9 (top), 26; AP Photo/Barbara Kinney/White House, p. 9 (bottom); © The London Art Archive/Alamy, p. 10; © iStockphoto.com/Global Photographers, p. 11 (main); © Jszg005/Dreamstime.com, p. 11 (inset left); © Jerry Shulman/SuperStock, pp. 11 (inset right), 13; © Alvey & Towers Picture Library/Alamy, p. 12 (top); © Creo77/Dreamstime.com, pp. 12- 13; © Ben Radford/CORBIS, p. 14 (left); © Ryan McVay/Photodisc/Getty Images, p. 14 (right); © GK Hart/Vikki Hart/The Image Bank/Getty Images, p. 15 (top); AP Photo/Alan Diaz, p. 15 (bottom); © Purestock/Getty Images, p. 16; © Vicky Kasala/Digital Vision/Getty Images, p. 17 (top); © iStockphoto.com/AngiePhotos, p. 17 (bottom); © Justin Paget/Dreamstime.com, p. 18 (left); © age fotostock/SuperStock, pp. 18-19; © Rick Diamond/Getty Images, p. 19; © Andersen Ross/Photodisc/Getty Images, p. 20; © Adrian Green/Photographer's Choice/Getty Images, pp. 20 -21; © WILDLIFE GmbH/Alamy, p. 22; © Arthur Tilley/Taxi/Getty Images, p. 23; © Tammy Mcallister/Dreamstime.com, p. 24 (1st from top); © April Turner/Dreamstime.com, p. 24 (2nd from top); © iStockphoto.com/orix3, p. 24 (3rd from top); © Peter Cade/Iconica/Getty Images, p. 24 (bottom); © GK Hart/Vikki Hart/Photodisc/Getty Images, p. 25 (left); © Marta Johnson, p. 25 (right); © Larry Prosor/SuperStock, pp. 26 -27; © Jetta Productions/Walter Hodges/Getty Images, p. 27; © Barbara Peacock/Photographer's Choice/Getty Images, p. 28; © David Young-Wolf/Photographer's Choice/Getty Images, p. 29 (top); © James L. Stanfield/National Geographic/Getty Images, p. 29 (bottom).

Front cover: © Gandee Vasan/Stone/Getty Images.
Back cover: © iStockphoto.com/syagci.